Losing Siggie

A Passage Through Grief,
in Poems and Photographs

JENN LYONS

Losing Siggie
A passage through grief, in poems and photographs

Copyright © 2019 by Jenn Lyons

All rights reserved. No part of this publication may be reproduced or transmitted in any form or by any means, electronic or mechanical, including photocopy, recording or information storage and retrieval methods now known or to be invented, without the written permission of the publisher, except by a reviewer who may quote brief passages in a review.

ISBN 2370000766434

Book design by Deanna Washington
Cover design by Doug Baird Productions and Deanna Washington

Photography:
Front cover photo by LexMex Photography
Back cover photo by Scott R. Kline
Scott R. Kline, pages 7, 11, 55
LexMex Photography, pages 50 and 52

Published by Josi's Paw Dog Walking and Pete the Pug Productions

For information, contact the author at jenn@josispaw.com

Printed in the United States of America

In honor of my co-pilot, Siggie.
June 19, 2006 to May 15, 2019.

In memory of my friend Gregory Johnson,
who loved dogs and loved helping his friends
with worthwhile causes.

And in memory of sweet Pete, pictured with Siggie
on many pages of this book. Pete passed away just as this book
came into print. He lived a beautiful life and comforted us always,
but especially in the six months after Siggie's death. His loss
marks the end of an era that will never be forgotten.

*"Goodbyes are only for those who love with their eyes.
Because for those who love with heart and soul
there is no such thing as separation."*
~ Rumi

Introduction

I've been a dog walker in San Francisco since 2008. I created my business for several reasons. It started as a memorial for a dog named Josephine that I lost in 2006, and then became a "purpose" for Siggie, the dog we adopted in 2007 who needed exercise and a job to do.

Before moving to San Francisco, I was working in a corporate setting and regretted not being able to spend the time I wanted with Josephine before her life was cut tragically short at the age of three. I had never held a job I felt passionate about, and really wanted that experience. Life is too short to be doing something you aren't truly ignited by.

My dog walking business has been a source of meaningful connection to Siggie and to many other dogs I have met through this work. I've spent so many special moments with dogs, providing happiness and love, and when their time on earth is done, saying goodbye. It's always hard when that day comes.

Losing Siggie has represented many things to me: The death of my best friend. Trying to find purpose again in the work we did together and loved. Understanding and living with the depth of pain from this loss. Being able to get out of bed again. Feeling like I can still find ways to be happy. And learning I can keep my heart open to love again.

Writing the poems and passages in this book was incredibly cathartic. I've never been a writer or poet. When Siggie died, words started coming to me in a way that had never happened before, and I started writing them down. After I had passed through the biggest waves of my grieving process, I felt inspired to turn these writings into a book.

It is my hope that through this book you will find comfort in knowing you are not alone in your grief. Losing an animal companion cuts deeply. Our pets are with us in the places and spaces of our everyday lives that other people often are not: getting out of the shower and drying our hair, taking out the garbage, unloading the groceries, waking up in the morning and making our bed, emptying the dishwasher, crying after a long day when we're feeling stressed. And our animals comfort us. They lick away our tears. They help us feel like everything is going to be OK. In my experience, this kind of vulnerability does not exist in any other form or relationship. It's OK to take the time you need to grieve deeply. There are many people who understand the profoundness of your pain.

The animals in our lives are here for only a short time. But the imprint they leave will last forever.

This book is dedicated to the sweet memory of Siggie and every other animal you and I have been lucky enough to share our hearts with. Our animals will always be a part of us.

The Story of Siggie

In November of 2006 my husband and I lost our three-year-old pug, Josephine, to a rare genetic illness that our local vets couldn't diagnose. We were in Colorado visiting my family, and she was with our dog sitter and good friend. Things happened quickly and she passed before we were able to return home. It was horrible. I remember walking to the park down the street from where my parents lived, flooded with grief and sadness. I looked up and saw a dog in a cute spiked collar, with a long body and short stubby legs. I asked the owner his name. "Harley," she said. I had never seen a corgi before, and I remember two things: his ears and his smile.

Soon after we got home, I began browsing online to investigate the breed and any corgis that might be close to our Chicago residence. I came across a six-month-old pup named Siggie that wasn't able to be shown due to her petite size and right high-hanging fingernail. She was a singleton puppy in Michigan with big eyes. I was hooked. I told my husband I was renting a car and driving up with my girlfriend to get her. It was winter and a big snowstorm was on the way, so my husband, thinking of my safety, volunteered to go get her. He was working in sales and had business in the area. I didn't argue.

The night he picked her up she rode alongside him in her crate, quiet and composed. As soon as he parked the car in our Lakeview neighborhood, I came down to meet her and she let out her first bark. It was the first of many in the next twelve-and-a-half years.

I have to confess, I didn't warm to her right away. She was way different from our pug. I didn't really understand what it meant for a dog to be a "working breed," or that she was used to a life in rural Michigan. She was nervous about the city lights, shy around new people, and not cuddly. I wasn't sure we'd made the right choice.

After my husband's job led us to San Francisco, our upstairs neighbor and friend mentioned needing someone to walk her five-pound Yorkie, Lily. It sounded like fun and a good opportunity to spend time with my dogs, too. (We had added a pug named Pete to our family shortly after getting Siggie.) So I said yes.

Looking back, I realize that dog walking was the job Siggie was born to do. We steadily built our client base and got a car to make pick-ups. We drove around the city and Siggie rode shotgun. She demanded it.

She was a horrible car barker. Her sense of hearing was so keen that whenever I shifted into reverse to park, she went ballistic. In the early years this drove me nuts. I tried so many things to make her stop. And then we figured it out. Treats at every stop, turn off the ignition and unbuckle my seatbelt at the same time so there would be only one sound instead of two. And let her sit up front to see everything.

She was the kind of dog that knew sounds in a way I've never observed in another dog. She knew that when you said "hello" or "goodbye," it meant there was going to be activity and movement, which would require barking. She knew the sound when you picked up your keys to leave. She recognized the sound of our car before it even pulled into the garage. If we ordered a Lyft or Uber, she knew the sound of the chime on our phone meant the car had arrived. Of course all of this resulted in more barking and management. It used to drive me crazy, and despite an array of dog trainers, nothing worked. The girl just wanted to bark.

I can't pinpoint exactly when, but somewhere along the way we reached a sweet spot, where I just allowed her to be the dog she was. I'd wave at neighbors instead of saying a verbal hello. When a repairman came by, we'd put her in a crate in my car to keep her calm. When friends brought their kids over, we'd gate her. I got to know our postal workers and convinced them she wasn't a threat.

Over the years we grew closer. She was the dog I could cry with, laugh with, fetch with. We both were always moving and were equally neurotic. She would follow me and help me with things like laundry, cooking, stretching after my run, and getting showered and dressed. We'd pack the dog walking bag together each morning with treats and all the essentials to start our day.

One of my favorite things about Siggie was that if we were staying in and having a movie night at home, I would go to the dresser and pick out a pair of comfortable stretchy pants to put on. She would come over and sniff them right away, as if she understood that wearing these pants meant I would be staying in for the night and we would be together. Then she'd let out a huff, throw her snout in the air, and grab a toy. She was always about the celebration.

Siggie was the hardest working dog I've ever known. And the most loyal and intelligent. It has been incredibly challenging to understand how to keep things going without her. She was a dog that couldn't be silenced, commanded the room, and just made you fall in love.

I think most of all what I will never forget is the way she could look at me and make me feel like the most important person in the world. Because of her I have realized that the most complicated relationships in life are often the most rewarding, and like anything truly wonderful, they change you forever.

I will always miss my sweet girl and barking queen, Siggie.

May 20

Sounds of the neighborhood waking up without you,
The birds outside,
Neighbors getting in their cars,
Other dogs barking.

I miss your morning energy,
Your toys squeaking,
Your footsteps up and down the stairs,
Your voice trying to manage everything happening inside and out.
It's hard to know what to do now.
I don't want to let you go but I know I must keep going.
I want you to stay fresh in my mind and heart forever.

I wish I could pet you,
Kiss you,
And tell you that you are my girl.
I miss that spot under your chin that I used to rub,
The area on your head between your ears that was so soft.
I miss the stubbiness of your paws.

I just miss you.

You are my heart and I ache for you.

May 28

I look at your bed and you're not in it
I come around the corner and your eyes aren't waiting
I open a door and I don't hear your voice
I get out of bed and you're not there to greet me

There is so much emptiness where your life once was.

How did this energy leave?
Did I dream it was there?
You seem so far away and I can't come with you.

How is it over?

How are you gone?

May 29

Grief — two weeks in:

The intentions are good, but no one can ever understand another person's loss.

Keep busy
    Drink
        Distract yourself
            Meditate
                Think positive
                    Do memorials
                        Fall back into society

But for what?
To wake up and have each day be something new but never the way it was?

When does grief lift?
When a smile comes out of sadness?

When do you forget what it was like to know yourself? Or do you settle into this new way of being? Knowing you can never go back. But you have to move forward.

Life doesn't slow down.
Sadness doesn't make time stand still.

I wish it could just freeze.

Don't let me forget.
Don't rush me.

Don't make me say goodbye. I'm holding on to the point of clinging, not to let go.

May 29
Knock at Your Door

"Knock, knock.
It's me, telling you life has to go on.
No more sitting it out,
Being absent,
Dwelling in your sorrows.
There is no advice, just love.
No easy fix, just time.
Get up, even though mornings look different.
Go to bed, though nights will never be the same.
Forgive yourself.
Rest yourself.
Keep your heart open."

May 30

There's this weird part of you, when you're going through loss, that you want to claim as personal outrage.

No one else can understand the depths of this life-altering absence.

Pain erupts from every pore. My mind keeps repeating, "No one else has ever had a bond this close. No one else knows what it feels like to be so ripped open and torn apart."

Some of us get to be with our animals at home. Others have to say goodbye at the vet's office. Some of us don't get to say goodbye at all.

No matter the context, there is no differentiation between the hurt that lingers after a life is over and the many years of love that have been expended in the relationship.

We all feel the depths of this collective heaviness.

June 3

There's already this new normal setting in that I can't stand.
Where we make do with the places you aren't, and go on about life.

Your ashes are displayed,
Your paw print is up,
Your toys and bed remain untouched.

Three weeks in.

Part of me feels like I should accept it.
That I need to.
Because at this point, nothing will bring you back.
We're making do but I don't like it.

I'm honestly not sure what to do. Grief has never grappled with me in this way.

I can't bring myself to get out of bed and have my feet touch the floor the way they used to; I know your kisses won't be there to greet them.

I'm struggling to stand on solid ground without you.
But I'm trying to be brave.

June 3

Work.
It happens each day like it always has.
The sunlight comes in and we get up and pack our bag.

I have a new front seat passenger now and you would approve. You grew up together and balanced each other. Pete is doing his best.

The days are the same in the motions, but so different.
Less excitement and noise.
A solemnness to the whole thing.
I don't think any of us know the meaning of work without you.

I miss the barks,
the complication,
the love.
The very essence of you.

Pete and I are holding you in our hearts and trying to find the strength to stand tall.

June 3

I look at your bed and it's so empty.
What I wouldn't give to see you.
The way you would lay with your head hanging off the bed and let out a big sigh.
You'd wait for me to go upstairs at night.
We'd finish our glass of red wine,
shut off the lights
and nestle in.
I could wake during the night and see you whenever I wanted.
It became instinctual.

I can't put your bed away just yet.
Leaving it out might bring Pete comfort, and it's a nice dream to imagine you're still next to me.

June 7

Sometimes I feel like I'm in danger of forgetting the vision of you.
To feel your spirit and look forward to your sounds.
This new normal isn't my choice but I don't know how to fight it.
I haven't been able to let you go.
I look at the spaces you've been but I can't see you.
As hard as I try.

I just want to lose it.
Go into a full rage and demand we can be together again.
But I know that's not the way it works.

We can only hold on until we have to let go.

June 20

A day after your birthday and almost two weeks out of town. We took a trip to Colorado, where we as a family were planning to celebrate your thirteenth birthday.

We scattered your ashes in the mountain streams, on top of wildflowers, on beautiful rocks and in the roots of tree trunks.

I somehow came to terms with things. And, at times, felt an acceptance.

Now that I'm back home, looking at the spot you used to lay, it's almost as if time stood still.

The first thing I did when we walked through the door, back from our travels, was wash your bedding. Making a step in moving forward.

But now, as I get ready to go to sleep, I find myself bringing your ashes up to the bedside.

I need your comfort next to me.

June 20

Being away was diverting.
A change of scene, a change of routine, and no memories of the places we had been together.
                    Except that I thought of you everywhere.
                            Even the places we had never been.

Getting up in the morning was different.
No consciousness about where my feet would touch the ground, and going without your kisses.

Sometimes I think I'm getting used to life without you.
                And I don't want to.
                            But I'm not sure what else to do…

June 23

I hope I'm not forgetting you.
Time is doing this weird thing where it's moving forward and I'm going along with it.
I'm learning to live in this place and space without you.
It's been almost six weeks since you passed.
Our business that we built together is struggling. I came back after the trip to Colorado and lost two clients and another lead I had.
Is it a sign?
Was the reason I survived and thrived because of you?
It's hard not to feel defeated. You gave me purpose.
I'm hoping to find what that all means now.
I miss you.
I miss your nail clicks and all your sounds.
I miss your kisses.
I miss what it meant to look at you before going to bed and see a full space.
There is no fullness in this new place.

June 23

Did I dream you or were you really here?
The absence of life in the places you were makes it feel like it was all a concoction of my mind.

I still want to see you.
Sometimes I think I still feel you.
Maybe that's hope.
And memories of the times that once were.

You've left this space that's so silent. And so loud in its void.

We all miss you.

The house doesn't run as it should or did.

But still, we get up, have coffee, and figure out how to move through the day.

It's a new way of being.

June 23

I scatter you to take you to all the places we've been
                                     and all the places we've never been.
This way we can keep walking together.

I want to bring you everywhere because you are my heart.
I also want to keep some of you to myself, in your little box with your engraved name.
Sharing you and keeping you close.
You are everything.

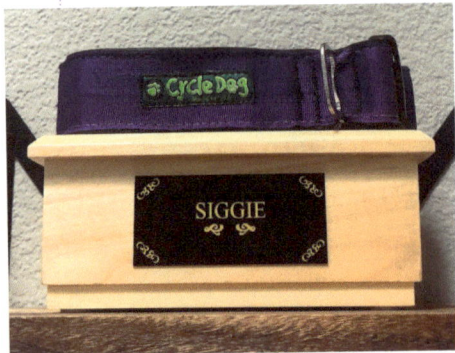

June 24

"I still have to sit with this, don't I?"

When your loss first happens your phone keeps ringing,
your email keeps updating,
things are lively…
You can't keep up.
You figure out you have a lot of support. So many good friends and deep connections.

"I still have to sit with this, don't I?"

Time goes by, society does its thing where there's an expiration date for your sadness. Not out of conscious awareness or cruelty, but just because that's how life is.
We keep moving…

"I still have to sit with this, don't I?"

No matter how I try to shake this feeling, it's still there.
Can I just flip a switch on sadness?

"I still have to sit with this, don't I?"

And you sit, and sit, and sit…
When do the pieces come back together?
When is there a golden adhesive that brings every broken part of you back into one?

"I still have to sit with this, don't I?"

June 27

I can still hear you scratch on the door as it opens.

I come out of the bathroom after getting ready for bed and expect to see you there, in your bed. Sometimes asleep, sometimes awake only to the point that your ears are waiting for me while the rest of your body lies still.

How can I shake these images?
And do I really want to?

You were my once in a lifetime, soulmate girl.
My memories of you play on repeat.

I think I don't know how to let you go.
I want to heal but I don't want to shake these beautiful images of you.
You are the beat of my heart.

Please don't stop.

June 28

Forty-four days.

Somehow, I didn't think I'd make it to today. Forty-four days since we said goodbye and I'm still here.

I remember getting the phone call saying you were gone, driving to the vet hospital like I had survived a massive trauma.

The only thought in my mind seeing you and holding you for the last time.

I had to get there and admit to myself it was real.

I somehow arrived accident-free and walked into the room, the doors covered with curtains on both sides.

The number on the door said Exam Room 6 –

My lucky number.

I sat down with Pete and the tech came in and told me a whole bunch of things I didn't hear. She looked sad.

Then she wheeled you in on a cart, covered in white.

I drew back the blanket, saw your head, and started wailing. The kind where you can't catch your breath and the hot tears stream down your face so fast you can barely see.

"I'm so sorry
I'm so sorry
I'm so sorry."

The only words I could repeat over and over until I felt like I had a chance at forgiving myself for leaving you there and making you go through any discomfort.

I picked you up off the cart, your body immediately limp in my arms.

I sat down and held you, hugged you, felt your fur against my face. You were still warm, you smelled the same, your fur still fresh and clean from the last bath I gave you a week ago.

It was you in my arms, but it wasn't you.

All the life had left your body and what I was holding was the vehicle.

Your 24-pound body had never felt so light in its heaviness.

June 29

I keep looking at the places you were.
It seems like too long to be considering that you might be there.
But I still hope,
I still miss,
I still long.

Please say it isn't over.
Nothing can fill the empty space that is you.
I keep trying to move forward.
Sometimes that angers me. Sometimes it confuses me.

Nights without you are lonely, days without you are silent.
Life continuing on is infuriating.
I wish there was a logical way to make sense of it all.
At this point I'm turning myself over to heartbreak.

I still see you,
I still understand and love every ounce of who you are.
I wish I could dial back everything.
I'm thinking of you tonight and the many spaces you filled in my life.

July 1

How am I getting to this other side?
Slowly...
Allowing myself to go back into the places I've been and covering myself in their blanketed layers.

If I don't think too much, adaptation becomes a natural instinct.
But then I think of all the years, how far I've come as a result of love and patience and complete vulnerability.

There was a journey —
That isn't forgotten when things change, when life moves on and coping is all you're left with.

In a blink, things end.
But, for a time, I was getting endless blinks from your beautiful eyes.

I miss you, Siggie.

July 2

There's this weird thing loss does to you.
You quit caring about time and its demands.
About what people think.
You struggle with knowing what to do for yourself to heal.

Do you make a big change?
Get away for a while?
Adopt a new animal?
Be patient with the way events and circumstances are lining up and take your time?

I wish there was a legitimate substitute for pain instead of distraction.
"Time heals all wounds."
But what do we do until time gets here?

July 23

There's no way to avoid starting over.
But does a new bond have a chance?
Does the old bond remain the thing you want to hang onto?
And can you do both?
So many emotions have come up in the past two weeks.
I feel like I have to expedite my feelings.
I like the space of your bed being filled with this new animal, but I also hate it.
I can't help but compare,
I can't help but feel lost,
I can't help but feel frozen.
Soon a decision has to be made. Do we say yes or no? Is she the right fit?
How should I proceed? Everything I've known has been altered.

Is there a way to stabilize among the noise of the clatter?

Or do I let the sound shatter everything?

July 29

I'm on edge about everything.
Going down new roads that are unfamiliar and unsteady.
Faced with choices I'm not sure how to make.
Frustrated with the things loved ones are doing or not doing.
Being without you.

It's a strange place, this new normal.
Nothing looks the same.
Yet, there's part of me that keeps expecting it to.

I look at our pictures and remember.
I go through my days and sometimes try to forget.
It's too tender.
It's too sacred.
It's too encompassing.

I miss that thing that I was when I was with you.

That thing is me.

August 6

This creature we have in our house right now, she's not you.
But she's bringing comfort.
I think starting with an innocence and youth is helpful.
She's figuring things out.
She's used to a different home life.
She's playful and a little nervous.
I'm not sure what dog she'll become.
I like that sense of mystery.

When we first got you, you showed a fear of people, fear of headlights on cars, a bit of a withdrawn persona that intrigued me.
I never would have guessed you would become who you were.

She doesn't bark much, but I like knowing that's your legacy.

There was one you, one us, one period that was just our own.
This is another chapter.

I think I'm looking forward to another storyline, while holding the one that was ours incredibly close.

August 16

You have become a passing ship in the night,
A memory I hold dear,
A story long been told.
All of the mindsets I need to cope with your loss.

I still have your fur around me,
Your picture next to me,
Your influence and purpose in my heart.

I wake up more,
My sleep is restless.

I already am moving my life forward with the absence of you in it.

It's not a choice…
It's the only way to keep breathing.

August 19

How is it possible our chapter is done?
Has everything already been written?

At first I was desperately trying to fill your space so I wouldn't let the pain in.
Now I just want to keep that space----
I want to make it bigger.

There isn't a way to fill it.
I'm lost,
I'm restless,
I'm sad.

Tonight I put my laundry basket in the space you used to sleep. Then I moved it.
Now I look at the emptiness, and the subtraction of an object doesn't make me feel any better.
Your absence burns.
Our love remains all around. In every room of this house.

How do we cope with the death of a soulmate?
How do we keep going when our heart wants to stand still?

I long for your eyes,
your snore,
your safe watch over me.

What I wouldn't give to turn back time.
Your love made me whole. I want to swim in your spirit.

August 23

Your features were beautiful:
eyes that could stare right into me
ears that responded to every motion and sound
a presence so large in a body only a fraction of its impact.

You still click your nails in every footstep in the center of my heart.
You still fetch in a way so dedicated it's in a league of its own.
You still bark even when all I hear now is silence.

You haven't left.

August 23

One of these days I'll get my balance back.
I'll understand what it's like to feel whole again.
I'll quit looking at the spaces you were and only seeing the void.
But I'm not there yet.
I don't know when I will be.

All I know is that I'm still mad at the way things have to be.
I don't want to be encouraged to propel forward.
I still want the past.

I want every last look at you before your light went out.
I want to add a flame back to the part inside me that feels cold and dark.

How I long for warmth…

September 8

You are still a part of me.
Over sixteen weeks without you.
My pain has lessened but sometimes unexpectedly comes back with a vengeance.

This is loss.
This is grief.
This is life.
There is no right or wrong way.

I've sat with feelings I didn't think would ever alleviate.
I still bring your ashes to bed when I'm missing you. I still talk to you when I feel like there is something I want to tell you. I still drive around with your harness hanging on my rear-view mirror.

These things bring me comfort. You bring me comfort.

I know that I would never be who I am in life without you showing me the way to truly live.
Your love has made me better, stronger, more vivacious.

I will continue to live for as long as I have left with your spirit guiding me. Thank you for the best days of my life and for inspiring me to keep creating more.

I will never forget you, sweet Siggie. Thank you for making me complete. And for letting me see the soft side of you that was your best kept secret.

Acknowledgments

This book would not have been possible without the generosity of the following people:

Gregory Johnson, Casie Gambrel, Fred Zirdung, Pamela Lyons, Bill Wilkinson, Karla and Gene Lipp, Natalie Lyons, Pamela Del Rio, Betty Carmack, Chantel Garrett, Patty Mok, Michaela Hug-Nelsen, Saad Ansari, Mimi Moncier, Eric Lundy, Craig Hermes, Melanyann Garvin, Anna Marie Ware, Kristi Cheek, Chad Stose, Emma Kershaw, Andre Lucero, Ann and Craig Swenson, Liza Sperling, Larry Lee, James Jackson, Nari and Michelle Ansari, Gabe and Dawn Longoria, John O'Leary, Sharon Donnelly, Nicole Hanusek, Akshobhya Mann, Amy Richardson, Aki Ichizuka, Charla Rodney, Ebru Tontas, Eric Bollman, William de Ryk, Winnie Tsou, Molly Fowler and Tyler Cookson, and Morgan Rossi.

I would like to acknowledge the amazing support of my husband, Brad, who has always encouraged any dream of mine I've wanted to chase. Thank you for lifting me up.

About the Author

Jenn Lyons lives in San Francisco, where she has had a successful dog walking business, Josi's Paw, since January 2008. She was inspired to leave a corporate job and go out on her own after the loss of her first dog, Josephine. Recovering from the loss was not easy. It took years for Jenn to come to terms with her pain. She realized that deep loving relationships with animals can be some of the most fulfilling in life, and among the most agonizing to rebound from when they end.

In spring of 2008 Jenn became a certified pet loss counselor through the Association for Pet Loss and Bereavement and began assisting in an SPCA pet loss support group led by Dr. Betty Carmack. As her wounds healed, Jenn found herself living an inspired life devoted to animals.

In 2019, after a six-month battle with stage 4 lymphoma, Jenn's dog Siggie succumbed to the disease just a month shy of turning thirteen. The book *Losing Siggie* is a piece of Jenn's heart. She shares the story of her grief, with love and with hope that this book will comfort others who have had a similar experience.

Jenn spends her days outdoors, walking up and down the beautiful hills of San Francisco in the company of many fine canines. San Francisco will always be Jenn's home. It's where she learned to follow her heart and believe that she could do anything. In her spare time Jenn enjoys cooking, running, yoga, talking to the local baristas, and taking her dogs to brunch.

You can contact Jenn at jenn@josispaw.com.

www.ingramcontent.com/pod-product-compliance
Lightning Source LLC
Chambersburg PA
CBHW040738150426
42811CB00064B/1784